Serving a Nation Divided:
Eleven Days in the Militia During the War of the Rebellion

Being a Journal of the

"Emergency" Campaign of 1862

by
A Militiaman

BLUE MUSTANG

P R E S S

Blue Mustang Press
Boston, Massachusetts

First printing

ISBN 978-1-935199-06-9
PUBLISHED BY BLUE MUSTANG PRESS
www.BlueMustangPress.com
Boston, Massachusetts

Printed in the United States of America

Introduction to this Series of Books

This series of books, "Serving a Nation Divided" seeks to offer contemporary views of historical events in the armed forces active during the American Civil War. These will largely be regimental histories of the various armies from both the Union and the Confederacy.

There is a great wealth of histories, recollections, regimental diaries, and other such types of published works relating to the people and operations of the American Civil War that were written by the then-living doers of those deeds. The surge in such writings, starting immediately after the War's end and peaking in the early years of the 20th century (when these writers were facing their own mortality) has left us with countless stories and lists of compatriots who did not make it home. This series hopes to bring many of those texts back to those who find interest in them, both on an entertainment level and on a research level.

It is often obvious that many of these works were written when time was growing short for those who had served on both sides. Thankfully, someone would feel that the author's story was one worth telling. As the Civil War now serves to remind us of our strength as a nation, it is important to know the histories of those who fought on both sides.

The histories often slide into personal recountings of events-and are stronger for it. This first book in this series is one such account. It was a brief period (indeed, 11 days!) in a very long war, but it is told with an immediacy that provides the reader with an opportunity to look back with amazing clarity.

It is often said that history is written by the victors. This series strives to demonstrate that when the aim is to remember those who fought and died, the agents of history are made safe by those who honor their service and sacrifice.

Originally published in 1883 by:
Collins Printing House, PHILADELPHIA.

Serving a Nation Divided:
Eleven Days in the Militia During the War of the Rebellion

Being a Journal of the

"Emergency" Campaign of 1862

by
A Militiaman
(Louis Richards)

INTRODUCTION

Twenty years have passed away since a band of hastily-gathered minute-men left their homes to defend the soil of Pennsylvania from the first threatened invasion of the State by the rebel army under General R.E. Lee. Viewed through the lapse of this long period, crowded as it has been with so many momentous events in the life of the nation, the incidents of that brief and comparatively unimportant campaign begin, nevertheless, from their increasing remoteness, to take upon themselves a degree of historic interest. In respect to both their significance and their adventure, they greatly exceed the occurrences which attended the march of the celebrated Advance Light Brigade to the defence of Philadelphia in the war of 1812-14, in which latter body of citizen soldiery the county of Berks had the honor to be liberally represented.

With many of the participants in the movements of September, 1862, that minor undertaking comprises the sum total of their personal experience of military service during the entire ordeal of our country's conflict. To them, therefore, the memories of that period of excitement and alarm are invested with a peculiar interest—a sentiment which must to a degree continue to be shared by their descendants. In the belief that a narration of its details may serve to rekindle in the breasts of his surviving companions something of the enthusiasm which they originally inspired, the writer has been encouraged, after the lapse of nearly a generation, to undertake the pleasing and congenial task.

Fidelity to fact is at the least claimed for the present performance, which, devoid as it is of literary pretensions, may nevertheless be deemed not unworthy of an humble place among the contributions to the history of a stirring epoch in the annals of our good old

Commonwealth at the trying period of the nation's struggle. The basis of the narrative is a personal journal of the service to which it refers, kept at the time it transpired, the entries in which were dictated by the feelings and impressions of the moment. These impressions, it is to be remembered, were those of a simple civilian—one who felt little interest in the details of military service apart from the cause in which it is undertaken. Yet the relation may, from this very fact, commend itself the more to the friendly regard of his comrades, most of whom were at that period equally inexperienced in the proper discipline of the soldier. On the other hand, should it attract the notice of the veteran, it will doubtless serve to amuse him by comparison with his own experience amidst the greater perils of "grim-visaged war," which he is even yet so pardonably fond of recounting.

From what has been already advanced, it will be unnecessary to place any special emphasis upon the disclaimer which it nevertheless remains to make, that any possible object of applause is sought to be associated with the expedition which it is purposed to record. Very distinctly is the impression made at the time in the mind of the writer, preserved to the present, that in promptly proceeding to the scene of danger, the Pennsylvania militia were confronted with a more urgent incentive than that which animated the legions of brave men who had already gone forth to face the enemy on the distant battle-fields of the South. Our homes were threatened—the horrors of desolating war seemed likely to be brought to our very doors. The instinct of self-preservation effectually appealed to even the most unpatriotic hearts. No other honorable alternative was left but to go out to meet the hostile invader. Alarms often repeated, by night and by day, suggested the imminence of the danger. Others, with a more deliberate devotion to their country's cause, had volunteered for long periods of service. To fail to rally for the protection of our own firesides, with all their consecrated associations, would have been unworthy of the very lowest requirements of patriotism. The most abiding sentiment of those who were called to no severer military duty than the militia campaign of 1862, or that of the following year, must always be a heartfelt appreciation of, and gratitude for, the services of the brave veterans of the War of the Rebellion, to whose heroic deeds we are indebted for the preservation of our liberties, and the blessings of a reunited country.

But, justice to the minute-men of 1862 requires it to be said that, although in the light of subsequent events, the achievements of their brief campaign seem to sink into such comparative insignificance—so marked indeed that the very narration of them appears to savor more of humor than of valor—there were among their number multitudes who were animated by as warm a patriotism as that which burned in the breasts of their gallant comrades then already at the front—who were as ready as they to lay down their lives in defence of the dearest interests of freemen, and who, had the occasion presented itself, would have done equal honor to their country's service. It is not to be forgotten, moreover, that at the crisis when they marched to the rescue of the State, it could not be foreseen what was to be the issue of their mission, or how great the sacrifice which they might be called upon to make. It was cause for lasting gratification with them that their very presence upon the borders at the juncture when they appeared, and in the numbers in which they came, greatly contributed to encourage their brethren who were then passing through the heat and fire of the conflict, as well as to deter the progress of the invading foe. Raw and undisciplined as they undoubtedly were, who can now say that their prompt rendezvous at the centre of military operations did not signally aid the successful efforts of the army to turn backward the march of the enemy after the terrific shock which he received on the memorable field of Antietam?

L.R.
Reading, September, 1882.

ELEVEN DAYS IN THE MILITIA

After the reverses to our arms at the disastrous battles of the Second Bull Run and Centreville, in the latter part of August, 1862, and the retrograde movements of the Union forces in Virginia in consequence, the purpose of the enemy to follow up his advantage by endeavoring to take the Capital, invade the Middle States, and thus strike terror into the hearts of the people of the North, became immediately apparent. In the early part of September, war meetings were being held in Pennsylvania to raise the quota of the State in lieu of the draft then impending, in pursuance of the requisition of the President of the United States for three hundred thousand men. The Reserves had been called away to succor the hard-pressed army of McClellan, and the borders were left wholly unprotected at the inviting season of harvest. As a measure of precaution against the impending danger, Governor Curtin on the 4th of September issued a proclamation recommending the immediate formation of volunteer companies throughout the State, in conformity with existing militia laws, for home defence, and suggesting the closing of all places of business at 3 o'clock P.M. daily, in order to afford due opportunity for drill and preparation. On the next day, Mayor David McKnight of Reading, who was acting in that capacity in the place of Mayor Joel B. Wanner, then in the field as Major of the 128th Regiment of Pennsylvania Volunteers, also issued a manifesto, in pursuance of the spirit of the Governor's proclamation, requiring the assemblage of the citizens at certain places designated within their respective wards, for the organization of companies, and also the holding of daily drills from 4 to 6 P.M.

On the 5th, the rebel army under General Lee, comprising a force estimated at eighty thousand infantry, eight thousand cavalry, and one hundred and fifty pieces of artillery, crossed the Potomac at or near the Point of Rocks, and entered Frederick. Among its division commanders were Magruder, Walker, Anderson, A.P. Hill, Stuart, Longstreet, Ewell, and Stonewall Jackson. With the occupation of Maryland, matters reached an alarming crisis, and the imminent danger to Pennsylvania became at once evident. The boldness and celerity of the enemy's movements suggested the necessity for prompt action on the part of the State authorities. On the 10th of September, the Governor, acting under the direction of the President of the United States, issued another proclamation, as Commander-in-Chief of the militia, designated as General Order No. 35, calling on all the able-bodied men of the State to organize for its defence, and be ready to march to Harrisburg at an hour's notice, subject to his order. The companies were directed to be filled in accordance with the army standards of the United States, and as it was stated that the call might be sudden, the officers and men were required to provide themselves with the best arms they could procure, with at least sixty rounds of suitable ammunition, good stout clothing, uniform or otherwise; boots, blankets, and haversacks. The order further stipulated that the organizations would be held in service for such time only as the pressing emergency for the State defence might continue.

On the morning of the 11th, the rebel cavalry under Stuart entered Hagerstown, the southern terminus of the Cumberland Valley Railroad, six miles from the Pennsylvania line, the main body being about two-and-a-half miles behind, at Funkstown. The army of McClellan had in the meantime advanced to Poolesville. As soon as this intelligence reached Harrisburg, the Governor at 4 o'clock on the afternoon of that day issued General Order No. 36, calling into immediate service fifty thousand of the freemen of Pennsylvania, under the terms of the proclamation of the previous day, to repel the rebel invasion.

Immediately after the publication of the proclamation of Wednesday, September 10th, the work of forming militia companies in Reading was begun in earnest, the efforts that had been previously made in that direction not having been attended with much practical result. In the evening, the court-house bell was rung, and the building was rapidly filled. Mayor McKnight presided over the meeting. Dispatches were read indicating the approach of the enemy to the borders, and resolutions were adopted to organize companies forthwith in each of the wards. Many went directly from the meeting to the different places of rendezvous, and enrolled themselves for the State defence. There was not at the time a single full military company in Reading, all the troops enlisted for stated terms of service having already gone to the front. The night was one of much activity and excitement. Drilling was done in Penn Square to the inspiring accompaniment of fife and drum, which gave the town a decidedly warlike appearance. This exercise was continued daily and nightly until the militia had marched, and at no period during the entire war did the military enthusiasm of the people reach a greater height.

In the instruction of the troops, the manual of arms had to be omitted, for there were no guns. Officers had been hastily selected, and the commands in most cases given to experienced soldiers, whose services were in sudden and great demand. The fidelity of the men was accepted without any suggestion of the test of an oath. The companies recruited rapidly, and were not long in filling up to the standard. Their evolutions, which were conducted to a large extent in the open square, under the cover of darkness, were at times edifying to witness. As the battalions marched with sturdy tread up and down on either side of the central market-houses, collisions would now and then derange the symmetry of the forces. Frequent resort to unmilitary language on the part of the commanders was necessary to bring up the laggard platoons, and movements were habitually executed for which no precedent could have been found in either Scott or Hardee. But it was patriotism and not tactics that was uppermost in the minds of all, and trifling imperfections of military discipline were, for the moment at least, sunk out of sight in the sense of common danger.

Arms of all kinds were in urgent demand. Rifles and shot-guns, single and double-barreled, old and new; pistols of all designs, long and short, ancient and modern, together with some other unclassified implements of war, were brought out from their hiding-places, hastily cleaned and put in working order. Some of the men, when equipped for the march, were walking armories of miscellaneous weapons. The hardware stores were invaded in search of powder, shot, and ball. A gum blanket, with which in most cases an army blanket, or in default thereof, a pair of ordinary bed blankets, were rolled up; a haversack of canvas or oil-cloth, hastily put together at the saddler's, a tin cup, knife and fork and spoon, made up the rest of the equipment.

But it was the composition of the forces which lent to them their chief dignity and formed their most notable feature. There was no volunteering by proxy. No one at all able to contemplate military service thought of stopping to suggest the duty of his neighbor. Each felt the personal application of the call, and even to doubt one's fitness for duty was to expose himself to suspicion. All claims of business, public or private responsibilities, or professional or official duty had to yield to the necessities of the hour. Every interest was alike threatened, and no balancing of individual excuses could for a moment be tolerated. The women nobly seconded the appeal to arms, and assisted in the work of preparation. Personal and social distinctions were levelled, and in response to roll-call there appeared the lawyer, the physician, the preacher, the magistrate, the banker, the merchant, the manufacturer, and the railway official in his multifarious forms, side by side with the humbler civilian—all animated with patriotic zeal in the common cause.

Mayor McKnight, who subsequently himself joined a company named in his honor and commanded by Captain Nathan M. Eisenhower, on the 11th sent William M. Baird, Esq., to Harrisburg to keep the home authorities informed as to the arrangements for the calling out and reception of the Reading militia. On the evening of the 12th, Mr. Baird telegraphed that the companies should hold themselves in readiness to march, and a little later communicated an order from headquarters to Captain Franklin S. Bickley, who was in charge of the first company organized, and the only one then ready, for his command to leave for Harrisburg the next morning by the first train.

This company had its rendezvous in the second story of the building at the southwest corner of Fifth and Washington streets. Its roll originally contained 94 names, but the number of men who actually marched was but 64. Sergeant William H. Strickland was left behind to recruit the company up to the standard, and afterwards brought a few additional men to Chambersburg. The commanding officers were all of them men of some experience in military affairs, and proved themselves worthy of their positions. Captain Bickley had been a commissioned officer in the Pennsylvania Reserves; First Lieutenant Lewis H. Wunder was a veteran of the Mexican War; and Second Lieutenant Charles H. Richards, though never in actual service, had had a long connection with the militia before the war. In the ranks of the company were a few old soldiers, who were generally to be recognized by the coolness of their bearing.

At this point it will be appropriate to give the names of the seven companies which were raised in Reading, or its immediate vicinity, and left in response to the Governor's call, with the dates of marching and their regimental assignments. Several other companies were in course of organization in the city and county,

15

but the emergency had passed before they were ready to respond to the call:—

Fifth Ward Guards, Captain F.S. Bickley, 70 men, Company G, 2d Regiment; September 13.

Nicolls Guards, Captain Charles H. Hunter, 104 men, Company E, 11th Regiment; September 15.

McKnight Guards, Captain Nathan M. Eisenhower, 95 men, Company I, 11th Regiment; September 15.

Liberty Fire Zouaves, Captain William Geiger, 70 men, Company G, 20th Regiment; September 17.

M'Lean Guards, Captain Samuel Harner, 45 men, Company H, 20th Regiment; September 17.

Halleck Infantry, Captain Frederick S. Boas, 92 men, Company I, 20th Regiment; September 17.

Berks County Cavalry, Captain Samuel L. Young, 67 men, Independent; September 17.

At a meeting of Captain Bickley's Company, held on the evening of the 12th, the marching order was read, and it was directed that the company meet at the armory at 10 o'clock the next morning in readiness to leave. Its subsequent movements during the campaign are detailed in the journal which follows, and to which what has already preceded is but a necessary preliminary.

****

Saturday, September 13. According to orders, the company met at the rendezvous at 10 o'clock A.M. equipped for the march. The morning had been busily occupied in getting ready for the departure. The leave-taking with our friends had not been unmingled with feelings of solemnity, in view of the possibility that we might never see them again. The day was fine, and a large crowd of people congregated in the streets to see us off. On Penn Square, in front of the Provost Marshal's office, at the old Bell mansion, the pavement was blocked, as it had been for several days past, with applicants for exemption from the draft. The medical examinations were then in progress. We marched to the lower depot, headed by a band, and accompanied by the crowd. The company itself was wholly unprovided with music of any sort. Left by the regular morning passenger train for Harrisburg. In another car there was also a militia company from Pottsville, commanded by Captain David A. Smith, which had left home the same morning. All the men were in good spirits. Some amusement was afforded by a comparison of our accoutrements. The majority of the company were unarmed, and the only insignia of a regular military organization were the swords and sashes of the officers. The news by the morning papers still continued exciting. The army was said to be preparing to engage the rebels in Maryland, as no time was to be lost in checking their advance.

The trip was without incident. Arriving at Harrisburg at 1-½ P.M., we were formed and marched to the State Capitol grounds. A scene of great activity was here presented. The people seemed everywhere to be flocking to arms. The Governor and the Adjutant-General were personally superintending the organization of the militia. Secretary Slifer and Colonel A.K. McClure were also actively engaged in the same work. We were much relieved to find that we were to be furnished with arms and equipments by the State, as our force was far from effective in its present shape. At the State Arsenal, on the Capitol grounds, we were supplied with Springfield muskets, knapsacks, haversacks, and canteens.

Delivered up our old guns to be returned home. The muskets and bayonets, on first introduction, were handled with some curiosity. As there were no scabbards provided for the latter, the bayonets had to be carried fixed to the pieces. Of ammunition there was none on hand at present, but it was stated that a supply would be sent after us. Nothing was said about swearing us into service. The day was likely to be consumed in regimental organization, and it was probable we should not get off before the morrow. Some of our men had expected to meet the rebels before night. Fortunately for us, we still had some eighty miles the advantage of them.

The first charge was upon our bags of provisions. My haversack had been bountifully stocked by my good landlady at home, Mrs. B., whose liberality as a provider and kindness of heart will always be held in grateful remembrance by her guests. The foresight of the Governor in mentioning in his proclamation the subject of rations, was generally commended, as little or nothing eatable seemed to be obtainable in this town since its occupation as a militia camp.

Our company was assigned quarters on the east side of the Capitol grounds, upon the lawn in the rear of the public buildings. Passed the afternoon in watching the arrival of several additional companies, strolling around the Park, and looking through the Capitol buildings. Several of us climbed the stairway to the dome. Another charge on the haversacks about 5 P.M. Began to wonder where or how we were to pass the night. Our efficient Quartermaster, L.M.; at length solved the problem. He procured a lot of shelter tents, which were distributed, and the work of setting them up commenced. A little straw was brought from somewhere and put in for a bottom. Took a stroll through the town in the evening with Messrs. G., E., S., and others, visiting the railroad depots, which were just then scenes of particular activity. Stopped on the way at a lager beer saloon, which powerfully recalled home associations. Returned to the grounds and answered to roll-call about 10 P.M. Crawled into a tent with Dr. B. and J.R.K. A regiment or two was encamped around us. No military rules were as yet promulgated, and it was very evident that none were to be observed that night. Chaos reigned supreme. Singing, speech-making, and practical jokes of all kinds filled in the hours usually devoted to sleep, while the arrival of fresh companies, from time to time, appeared to stimulate the orgies as the night advanced. Slept a couple of hours, and until 2 A.M., when the general discomforts of the situation moved me to seek more desirable quarters. Reconnoitred the outskirts of the camp, and found a large covered coach just outside the grounds, which I got into, and having wrapped myself in my blanket, slept tolerably for several hours. The night was quite cool, and these new accommodations proved comfortable only by comparison. Got out at daylight, washed my face at a pump, answered to roll-call, and then consulted my bag of provisions. This first night's experience in "camp" suggests how few and simple are the wants of man in a military state.

Sunday, September 14. Went down town with Dr. B. to look after something to replenish our depleted commissary stores. The Doctor was acquainted with a family named Feger, in Walnut Street, near the river, whose son was a student of medicine, and suggested a call. We accordingly visited them, and were kindly provided with a good meal and a quantity of cigars. The young student conducted us to a bakery, where we laid in a supply of crackers. Returned to camp. Our company had been attached to the Second Regiment of Militia, as Company "G." The Colonel was John L. Wright, of Columbia. There were ten companies, mostly full, from Columbia, West Chester, Reading, Pottsville, and Lancaster City and County. The First Regiment, commanded by Colonel Henry McCormick, and containing companies from Harrisburg, Philadelphia, and Chester and Lebanon counties, had already been sent off down the Cumberland Valley Railroad to Chambersburg. At 11 o'clock we received marching orders for the same place, and about 1-½ P.M. the regiment proceeded out to near Camp Curtin and got aboard a train of freight cars, which had been provided with seats for the transportation of troops. A long delay, with the explanation of which we were not furnished, ensued; but about 3 the train started. A halt of an hour or more was made in town. A tremendous and enthusiastic crowd was out to see us off. Moved over the Long Bridge and stopped another half hour west of the Susquehanna. Chambersburg, our destination, was fifty-two miles distant. Passed successively through Mechanicsburg, Carlisle, and Shippensburg, at each of which places short stops were made. Were struck with the great natural beauty of the Cumberland Valley region. Crowds of people came out to the stations to meet us, and black and white, old and young, all joined in the heartiest demonstrations of welcome. Were also greeted from the houses and roadsides all along the line by people waving their handkerchiefs and swinging their hats. At Mechanicsburg a whole girls' school was out to see us. This was a specially engaging sight to some of our number, who thought that that village would be a good place to camp. At Carlisle I met Mr. R.S., whom I knew. The elite of the town were at the station, and S. pointed out to me the leading beauties of the place—I mean the ladies. Soldiers of a day, we already began, in the midst of these inspiring scenes, to feel like real veterans. Between stops the men beguiled the time singing, jesting, smoking, etc., and every one was in the best possible humor. Private T.H., among the rest, favored the company with a curious song in Pennsylvania Dutch called "Babbel Maul," which performance his delighted auditors compelled him frequently to repeat. It was generally agreed that the most desirable way of marching was by railroad. Dusk deepened into night, and at about 9 o'clock Chambersburg was reached. Proceeded a mile or two below the town, when the train halted in a wood brightly illuminated with camp-fires, and resonant with the cheers of soldiers. Disembarked and went into camp.

Rigged the tents, built fires, mounted the large cooking kettles with which we had been furnished at Harrisburg, boiled coffee and got our supper—"grub" is the military term for it. No news of any account from Maryland. My two comrades of the night before and myself constructed a sort of crib with fence rails put up between adjoining trees, and, after a smoke, laid ourselves up in it to sleep. The arrangement worked well, and we slept comfortably in this rustic bedstead until 5 A.M.

Monday, September 15. After roll-call wrote letters home, and carried some water for the cook. The latter, W.P.D., is a character in his way, and deserves mention. Under a rough exterior he carries a kindly heart. In his particular sphere, the importance of which we all recognize, he is somewhat of an autocrat. In the distribution of the eatables he is governed by the strictest principles of equity, and shows no favoritism. He is very often justly ruffled when his functions are usurped, or undue dictation is attempted on the part of those bearing higher official authority. He is specially incensed at times when stratagems are employed by the men to steal the sugar, over which latter article he finds it necessary to maintain a vigilant guard. We are now down to regular army fare, our bill consisting of rations of bread, meat, coffee, and that well-known item of camp necessaries called "hard tack," which is a host in itself, being made to go a great way by reason of the degree of mastication which it requires. There can be no complaint as to the strength of the coffee, since there is no milk to dilute it, but the color of the sugar might afford ground of exception on the part of the over-fastidious. Soups of rice, meat-bones, and occasionally poultry, when there happen to be any hen-roosts in close proximity, make a substantial dinner. Soldiers' appetites are uniformly good, and little defects in the system of cookery are not ordinarily closely criticised. Tobacco, in all its forms, seems indispensable, by reason of the moral courage with which it is supposed to inspire alike the soldier and the civilian. This article is laid in by the men whenever and as often as occasion presents. In our great country it has all sections for its own. It is certain that the war is going to give an immense permanent stimulus to the consumption of this standard narcotic. Alcoholic beverages also are stored away in flasks against cases of emergency, which, in military affairs, as is well known, are of constant occurrence.

During the morning we were gratified with the first sight of the enemy's paraphernalia, consisting of a train of captured baggage wagons, taken from Longstreet, and which were being driven in the direction of Harrisburg, whither, it is said, some hundred or more of prisoners from the same corps are being conducted. With a view of the latter we were not rewarded. The curiosity of the men to see a live rebel—in a captured condition—is very great. The wagons were guided by contra bands, who did not, however, look as if they belonged to the numerous class called "intelligent," who figure so largely as news-bearers in the army dispatches. The train, as well as the prisoners, was under the escort of the Anderson Cavalry, which was doing scout duty between the lines. A slight change in the position of our quarters was ordered during the day, and tents were struck about 4 P.M. and the company marched about two miles further to the south, halting in a large stubble field west of the railroad, in a position which had been dignified by the title of "Camp McClure." Had an attack of my old adversary, the sick-headache, and was soon forced to surrender. Was very kindly waited upon by several of the men, especially P.E. and his brother D., who is a candidate at home for District Attorney, but not on that account any the less unselfish in his friendly offices on the present occasion. The former made me some tea from pennyroyal, gathered upon the ground, which shortly operated as an emetic. On a bed of blankets and straw, arranged by sympathetic hands, with my knapsack for a pillow, and the open vault of heaven for a canopy, I soon became, as is usual with sufferers from this severe complaint, utterly indifferent to surroundings. A good night's rest brought a happy relief.

Tuesday, September 16. Part of the morning was devoted to foraging at the neighboring farmhouses, but little or nothing could be procured, the ground having already been pretty well covered by advance parties. Apples, however, were abundant, as there were many fine orchards in this vicinity. Was detailed to attend Dr. S., the Company Surgeon, who was sick, and had taken refuge in an adjoining wood, into which our quarters were presently moved. Here, under the direction of the Quartermaster, a sort of wigwam was constructed, built of fence-rails and cornstalks, and floored with straw. It was long enough to accommodate the entire company, and formed a very tight and really comfortable tenement. The Conococheague Creek ran within a few hundred yards of the camp, and the men had several good baths in it. Regiments were continually arriving from the railroad, and the shrieks of the steam-whistles, the blasts of bugles, clatter of drums, and the cheering of the troops enlivened the day. Among the accessions were the Blue Reserves, of Philadelphia, a uniformed organization, which made a handsome appearance. Before night there were said to be ten thousand men on the ground. A large force of militia was evidently intended to be concentrated at this point. Met a number of acquaintances among the new arrivals. Had several squad and company drills, and expected, from the arrangements we observed in progress, to remain some time in this situation. While out for exercise we could hear the noise of distant artillery proceeding from the direction of Sharpsburg and Harper's Ferry. The anxiety increased to hear something from the army. Occasionally a newspaper, a day or two out of date, was brought in from the railroad, and its contents eagerly devoured. It was said that Hagerstown had been abandoned by the rebels, and that telegraph and railroad communication had been re-established with that point. Reports circulated, which were afterwards verified, that fighting had commenced between the corps of Generals Hooker and Reno and the rebels, and that General Reno had been killed. When the camp-fires were lighted, after nightfall, the woods resounded with martial music, song, and cheers, and the scene was a highly animating and inspiring one. Such sights are seldom witnessed, and are not to be soon forgotten. Before turning into our hut, seated myself on a bank a little distance apart from the rest, in company with my friend K., and we took a quiet smoke and talked of home, whither our thoughts continually turned. Enjoyed the best night's rest of the campaign, owing to the comfort of our quarters.

Wednesday, September 17. Drilled in the morning in the adjoining fields, and while thus engaged observed a renewal of the reports of artillery towards the south, heard on the day previous, and with still greater distinctness. These proceeded, as we afterwards learned, from the battle-field of Antietam, some thirty miles off. A dull gruff belch, at irregular intervals, accompanied by a sense of concussion, told the story of the distant conflict. This inspired strange and solemn feelings. Human lives were being offered up as a sacrifice upon the altar of our country, and thousands of homes would sit in dread suspense until it should be known upon whom the fatal blows had fallen. The result, too, was of great concern to us, who were mere auxiliaries in reserve against an untoward crisis. The evolutions now assumed a significance they had not heretofore possessed. Their object seemed no longer to be skill merely, but preparation. The zeal for duty was quickened, and it was the idea of responsibility which was uppermost in the minds of all. Additional regiments meanwhile arrived, among others two of the Gray Reserves and Home Guards of Philadelphia, which left Harrisburg yesterday. With drilling, guard mounting, and the usual routine of camp duties, the day wore slowly away. Another picturesque scene at night. After roll-call crawled again into our comfortable domicil of cornstalks, with every reason to expect another good night's sleep. This idea, however, was a grievous delusion, as the sequel will show.

Thursday, September 18. About 11 o'clock last night the beating of the ominous long roll aroused us from our peaceful slumbers, and the word quickly passed that we had received marching orders for Hagerstown, and were to be ready to leave at 12. The accoutrements having been collected by the light of the fires, the regiment marched to the railroad, a mile off, where it was expected a train would be in waiting for us. Alas! we here received our first practical lesson of the great uncertainty of military movements, and the mechanical nature of the duties of the soldier, who must obey orders, simply, without inquiring for reasons. In the quality of civilians, which we could not altogether consent to drop, our sense of individual importance was frequently infringed upon in our new capacity. Each in his turn felt disposed to divide with his superiors the responsibility of the command. After waiting several hours in the crisp cool air of the autumn night, without any train appearing, we lost all patience and lay down on our blankets for temporary repose. As the dews of heaven gently distilled upon our unprotected forms, the memory of the comfortable quarters we had just left did not add to the feelings of reconciliation to our present miserable situation. Sundry imprecations were vented upon the unknown authority in charge of the department of transportation. Many went to sleep, from which they would be occasionally roused by the rapid passing of trains, but our own looked-for conveyance did not, nevertheless, arrive. Morning broke at length and breakfast was improvised by the cooks.

We waited hour after hour for our train, but in vain. Wrote letters home beside the railroad track, on the ends of the sills. Various reports from the army were in circulation, respecting the result of the battle, and the movements of the enemy, subsequently found to be unreliable. After dinner had a battalion drill, and when all expectation of the train had been given up, between 3 and 4 o'clock it suddenly appeared. Cheers greeted its arrival. It consisted, like the one in which we had come down, of house cars adapted for the present purpose, and we boarded it just in time to escape a shower which began falling at this moment. Were off, at length, and after a short halt at Greencastle, where I laid in some provisions, arrived about 6 o'clock at Hagerstown, which we found occupied by a considerable militia force that had been pushed forward within the past two days. Were surprised to find the companies of Captains Hunter and Eisenhower, from Reading, already there, as they had started from home after we had. Were informed by them that they had left Harrisburg on Tuesday night, and arrived at Hagerstown on Wednesday morning. They had been attached to the 11th Regiment, to the command of which Charles A. Knoderer, a talented civil engineer of Reading, who went as a private of Captain Eisenhower's company, had been promoted. The regiment was encamped a short distance below town on the Williamsport pike. Heard more definite intelligence of the result of the great battle fought yesterday, which is claimed as a decided Union victory. Were informed of the death of Captain William H. Andrews, of the 128th Regiment, who fell in the battle, and also of its commander, Colonel Croasdale. Captain Andrews's body had already arrived in Hagerstown. Several other members of Reading companies had been killed.

Our company was separated from the regiment and marched in the dusk of the evening into a narrow lane not far from the railroad depot, where we were told we were to pass the night. The ground was wet from the rain which had fallen, and a slight drizzle continuing, a most gloomy and uncomfortable aspect was imparted to the surroundings. The prospect for rest was extremely unpromising. There was nothing to lie upon except our gum blankets, and no better shelter than what could be improvised by stretching the tents—with which we were now temporarily provided—from the top of a fence to the ground. There appeared to be some confusion as to the arrangements for quarters, and we could not understand why a better situation had not been selected for the night's bivouac. After supper K. and myself went through the town to buy some lanterns and other things for the quartermaster. We were conducted by an old negro whom we picked up by the way, and obtained what we were in quest of, as well as a couple of bottles of good whiskey, procured at a grocery store, notwithstanding the fact that the town was under martial law, and the sale of liquor to soldiers had been prohibited.

After having made a pretty thorough exploration of the place, we returned to quarters, where we found a sharp discussion going on as to the propriety of the Governor's sending us across the State line, the authority for which some of the men were disposed to question. The objection evidently proceeded from those who did not like our present proximity to the seat of war. The debate ended, however, in a tacit concurrence in the opinion of the majority that it was all right. Passed a miserable night in this uncomfortable situation. Slept but little, and caught a severe cold, from the effects of which I suffered for several weeks.

Friday, September 19. Orders came about eight o'clock to go into camp at a place about a mile below town, on the Williamsport pike, and in the course of a couple of hours the scattered regiment had been collected and transferred to the point indicated. The spot was known as the old Washington County Agricultural Fair Ground, and but a few days previously had been occupied as a rebel camp. Its principal attraction was a large and fine spring of pure water. The 11th was in the same vicinity. Before the company moved from the lane, I had been detailed, with a squad, to go to a certain farm-house, about two miles out of town, for the purpose of impressing a team for the conveyance of the regimental luggage. Went to the place designated, but found that the farmer's wagons were already in service—at least he so informed us. Lieutenant William P. Brinton, of Company H, and myself then proceeded half a mile further upon the same errand, and found a man plowing in a field. Told him that we wanted his team, and he complied without protest. I rode one of the horses to his house, and during this time heard some pretty heavy artillery discharges in the direction of the Potomac, or rather to the eastward, apparently about six or eight miles off. This was occasioned, as it was afterwards developed, by the escape of the main body of the rebel army across the river, below Williamsport, under a fire from detachments of McClellan's forces. After we had been kindly treated to a good lunch by the farmer, the team was conducted off in the charge of the lieutenant, while I took the nearest course to the farm-house first visited, to bring back some men who had been left there. Finding that they had already gone, I walked into Hagerstown, where I had some difficulty in ascertaining the whereabouts of our regiment, the marching orders having been executed during my absence. Took the opportunity to reconnoitre through the town for the purpose of laying in some provisions. The great frequency with which that occupation is noted in this narrative need excite no undue wonder, since, as we were nearly always eating, our private supplies were in a continually deplenished state. Hagerstown is an antiquated looking place, and is, at the present time, the seat of unusual activity, owing to its proximity to the centre of military operations. The population was said to be about equally divided in its political sympathies. It had been held alternately by both sides, so that everybody had had in turn an opportunity of "giving aid and comfort to the enemy." At the present it was transformed, for the time being, into a vast hospital, many of its public buildings being occupied for this purpose. Governor Curtin was here looking after the welfare of the Pennsylvania troops. By the Williamsport pike, a number of our wounded soldiers were still being brought in from the battle-field, a distance of ten miles. The sight of these sufferers was touching. Some were in ambulances, while others lay in the bottoms of ordinary farm wagons, with little or no shelter from the hot sun. Their wounds had been dressed, and the heroic courage which they manifested was something inspiring to witness. Many bodies of the dead had been sent in for transportation. In a wheelwright shop to which my attention was attracted, I saw the lifeless forms of two officers in uniform—a major and a lieutenant—awaiting boxing. The faces were ghastly, and I turned from them with a feeling of pain as I thought of the hearts that even now, perhaps, were being torn with grief in the distant homes. These sights were realities, not pictures, and gave me a more vivid idea of the horrors of war than the most graphic pen descriptions I had ever read. Alas! I thought, to what extent is this slaughter to go on, and when will the sacrifice for patriotism's sake be complete?

Came up with the camp at length, and found the men engaged in clearing the ground and pitching the tents, which work was continued until dinner time. Toward the middle of the afternoon, great interest began to centre upon the road, occasioned by the frequent and furious galloping up and down of cavalry pickets and aids, and the report spread that a considerable body of rebels was advancing up the pike in the direction of Hagerstown. The long roll was beat, and the command to fall in was given. We were now supplied with sixty rounds of ammunition per man—the first that we had received—and loaded our guns, which looked like business. In default of the usual appliances for that purpose, the cartridges were deposited in our overcoat pockets. Thus ballasted, we were marched down the road about a mile and a-half, and halted at a point where detached lines of battle were being formed. Our regiment was deployed in two ranks to the left of the great road, in a ploughed field, on rising ground, and was in the front line. The Gray and Blue Reserves of Philadelphia, supported by a battery, constituted a portion of the right wing on the other side of the road, and the Maryland Brigade, a uniformed body of three years' men, five thousand strong, commanded by General Kenley, were posted on our extreme left. A regiment of skirmishers were in a wood a little in advance of the brigade. Some twelve or fifteen thousand men were thus concentrated in several lines, and the whole force was so disposed as to afford a converging fire upon the road. Major-General John F. Reynolds, who we learned was in command, had his headquarters on a hill, to the right of the road, where the colors were planted, and at which point aids were observed to be constantly reporting.

Things now began to wear a serious appearance. A number of farmers were noticed removing their household goods from our front, towards Hagerstown, by the road. They were evidently alarmed, and expected a battle. It was also remarked that portions of the fences along the pike had been torn down, and the rails piled up at different points in the road, by way of obstructions against the advance of an opposing force. We stood at a rest in the line, with guns half-cocked and bayonets fixed, momentarily awaiting the appearance of the foe. An incident occurred at this juncture which, though trifling, drew the attention of the entire force for the time being. The report of a musket was heard in the woods where the skirmishers were, followed by a loud shriek and audible groans. It was at once surmised that one of the militiamen had been accidentally shot. Presently, a crowd was observed conducting a man up the road toward the town, and it was then explained that this person was subject to attacks of mania-a-potu, and that the excitement of the moment had made him crazy. The occurrence could not but be suggestive of a similar catastrophe to the reason of some others of the force, who were just then exposed to the like danger.

Our Colonel next rode along in front of the regiment, observing to us that we must not mind if we found a little hail coming over in our direction soon. The preparations were now complete, and the decisive moment seemed to be rapidly approaching. But—tamely enough to relate—hours were passed in the same situation without any further developments whatever. Meanwhile the beautiful autumnal afternoon wore gradually away, and the sun went down behind the Cumberland Mountains, throwing a flood of golden light over the really picturesque landscape. Virgil's charming line involuntarily crossed my mind:—

"Sol ruit interea, et montes umbrantur opaci."

The singular beauty of the scene, and the absorbing interest of the situation, with its profound and alternating emotions of hope and apprehension, painted a picture upon the memory which time can never obliterate. Dusk thickened into night, and we remained in a standing posture until nine o'clock, when we were permitted to rest our pieces upon the ground and stealthily eat our rations. Some neighboring grain-stacks were invaded, and a few sheaves brought, which we unbound and strewed along the clods. Upon these we were at length allowed to lie down to rest—not to sleep—still grasping our cocked pieces, and ready for an instant alarm. About one o'clock the report was circulated, which proved to be the fact, that the forces of McClellan had driven the enemy across the Potomac into Virginia; but it was stated that some detached bodies of the latter had been cut off, and that the services of the militia were desired in order to capture them. The proposition was discussed—a debate being admissible under the peculiar circumstances, since it will be remembered we were not sworn into service—and it was resolved that we would go as far as the Potomac. Before we could move, however, the order was countermanded, and the summons was now suspected to be a stratagem to test our mettle. But contemporaneous events justify the conclusion that it was otherwise, and that no ruse was designed to be attempted in this affair, at the expense of the gallantry of Pennsylvania's home defenders.

Saturday, September 20. At daylight we were allowed to break ranks and stack our arms. No very definite information could be obtained during the morning as to the probable developments of the day, but, so far as appearances indicated, the situation of affairs was unchanged.

While in our present position I cannot restrain a feeling of admiration for the earnestness of many of the members of our organization. Among them are some of Reading's most considerable citizens, men who occupy important stations, and carry weighty responsibilities. Strange figures, indeed, they make here, in far-off Maryland, resting upon their arms, and keeping watch for the invading foe. Could their loved ones see them at this moment, what moral heroes would they appear in their eyes! I could not help observing how strikingly the predominant characteristics of men are developed in critical emergencies. In our mutual concern for the common safety, it is in the strongest characters that we feel our chief reliance is to be placed. Those who have the fairest reputations at stake, display the greatest degree of firmness, and vice versa. This criterion, it is evident, will hold good when the severest test shall be applied. H.V.R., a member of the Bar, cares little for the details of military discipline, but is a model of fidelity to the idea of duty, as is also his brother J., who is a layman. Dr. M., a bank officer, is punctuality itself, probably from long force of habit, and shrinks from no service, even the humblest. His former connection with military companies makes him a highly intelligent soldier. Mr. G., also a lawyer—I waive the military titles—moves cautiously, deliberates and debates, but perseveres. As a gigantic shooting excursion he is probably best reconciled to the present expedition, and since we

have now secured our ammunition, is doubtless anxious to sight
the game. L.B., a merchant, is a model civilian, and a man of
recognized high character. He has left home with a purpose,
which he will stand to, come what may. D.E., the candidate for
office to whom I have before referred, was never born to be a
willing subject of rules in any sphere of life, and makes an erratic
soldier. He has become tired of the slow progress we have been
making toward the battle-field, which, in a spectacular sense, he is
impatient to look upon. J.W.B., a light-hearted old time captain of
a troop of horse, is true game; and the same may be said of our
Quartermaster, L.M., who keeps the command in good humor by
the jokes which he is constantly bandying with the Captain. J.K.S.,
printer, is remarkable for his intelligence as to the object of those
military manœuvres which the rest of us regard as inexplicable.
J.P. is a sturdy fellow, of clear grit, who would be a good neighbor
in a perilous moment. B.O. is a serious man, distinguished for the
quiet regularity of his bearing and steadiness of his movements.
Not so Dr. B., a waggish apothecary, whose skill as a forager I
have all along had occasion to mark, and who seems, when an
advance is made, to be at all points of the camp at the same time.
J.H.F., an ex-country justice of the peace, enjoys the distinction of
being the only man in the company in regimentals, having donned a
uniform made for him some years ago, when he was orderly
sergeant of a company which belonged to the Kutztown battalion.
His avoirdupois has greatly increased since the garments were
made, and his harness is so tight that he finds marching very
uncomfortable. He stands upright a large part of the time from
force of circumstances, and sits down with caution. Our orderly,
J.G.S., a harum-scarum young attorney, is a singular mixture of
discipline and drollery. Lieutenant R. is an exceedingly modest
man, who is not without knowledge and merit as an officer.
Lieutenant W. is an old soldier, of quick eye and firm bearing. The
utmost reliance can be placed in his intelligence and courage.
Private K., bank teller, before mentioned, and myself, though
separated in the ranks by reason of a difference in inches, have

taken a liking to each other, and have formed a solemn league of mutual assistance when matters come to the worst. As he is armed with a pistol and a dirk, in addition to his musket, I feel that the advantage of the covenant is largely on my side.

At 4 P.M. artillery firing was renewed in our front, and an hour or so later the long roll was again beat all along the line, and the command to fall in was given. A forward movement down the road had been ordered. The intelligence had been brought in that a body of the rebels had recrossed the river at Williamsport, and the subsequent official dispatches explained that this force was a detachment of Lee's cavalry under Stuart, with a regiment of infantry and some pieces of artillery, whose evident design was a raid upon Hagerstown, where a large quantity of military stores had been received for McClellan's army. General Couch's division had been sent up to drive him back, and it was the exchange of compliments between the two which we now heard, though of this explanation we were for the time being ignorant.

In the march down the road, the cavalry took the advance, and were followed by the Maryland Brigade. The militia then closed in, and the successive lines gradually dissolved into a single column. The musicians were sent to the rear. After proceeding half a mile or so, the column was halted, and came to a rest in the road, in which position it remained for an hour or more. By this time it was dusk, and the artillery discharges in the front had become really formidable. The firing was principally from the rebel guns. Signal rockets now and then illuminated the sky, and a brilliant panorama was presented to the view, the complexion of which was decidedly warlike. Aids galloped up and down the column at a rattling pace, and things rapidly assumed an air of confusion. I draw a veil over the scenes presented at this juncture among a portion of the reserves of General Reynolds. It would take a better soldier than myself to tell what would have been the result of a serious collision at this moment, to the body of this force, whose chief misfortune was that it was entirely undisciplined. The plan agreed on was to receive the advancing enemy with the bayonet, in case a fire should be found ineffectual to check his progress. Many of our comrades made leagues with each other, offensive and defensive, and examples of coolness and determination inspired confidence in the main body of the men, who, I am satisfied, would have followed orders and done their duty.

The firing presently ceased, and from some mounted officers the intelligence was communicated that General Couch's division was now immediately upon our front, and that our pickets were in correspondence with his. At about eight o'clock we were ordered to quarters in a stubble-field alongside the road, having been previously cautioned by the Colonel not to build large fires, which injunction, it is unnecessary to state, was faithfully obeyed. The roll was called by the orderly, and the guards posted for the night. Did guard duty from eight to ten, and from three to five. During the night, as the sequel showed, the enemy, finding their design anticipated, and perceiving the preparations on all sides to intercept them of so thorough a character, abandoned their project on Hagerstown, and, under the cover of darkness, quietly recrossed the Potomac, and escaped safely into Virginia—horse, foot, and dragoons! Thus virtually ended the militia campaign in Maryland.

Sunday, September 21. Moved our camp into a very desirable location in the adjoining woods recently occupied by our skirmishers. As it was now generally understood that all immediate danger was at an end, signs of the relaxation of military discipline began to appear, and we returned to the easy habits which had characterized our band of civilian soldiery before it arrived in the vicinity of the late scene of conflict between the hostile armies. The tents were leisurely put up, and, the strain of the past two days being taken off, we prepared to spend a pleasant day of rest in the cool shade of the woods. Some of the members of an adjoining regiment began a promiscuous firing of their pieces, which it was said came very nearly drawing down the fire of General Couch's guns upon our peaceful camp, it being supposed for the time being that some straggling bands of the enemy might still be lurking in the neighborhood. The chaplain of the regiment held religious services, while some of the men stretched themselves under the trees, and others made haste to write letters home, giving accounts of the perilous scenes through which they had passed. These missives, as it turned out, they had the gratification of delivering in person. The Quartermaster, with his accustomed forethought, had made a requisition before daylight on a neighboring hen-roost, and preparations for serving dinner had already been begun, when, at eleven o'clock, marching orders for Greencastle, Pa., arrived. This was an agreeable surprise, as it suggested a homeward journey. The authorities evidently regarded the emergency for which we had been called out as at an end, and since this fact was assumed, a longer sojourn in Maryland appeared undesirable.

We now packed up our traps and moved up to our former camping ground at the Agricultural Park, near Hagerstown, where the interrupted dinner of rice soup and chicken was most thoroughly appreciated. At two P.M. the regiment started off in light marching order, the baggage wagons following. We now took leave of the 11th, a portion of whom had been making themselves useful that morning in the town in unloading the military stores that had been sent here by rail for the army. As we passed through the streets, we put on our best appearance, the men struck up a song, and we were cheeringly greeted by the population. Reaching the open country, we marched at random. The afternoon was warm and the roads exceedingly dusty. About dusk, the line between Maryland and Pennsylvania was crossed, and three hearty cheers were given for the Keystone State. Stopped half an hour in the little village called Middleburg, or "State Line," at which point the Anderson Cavalry passed us on their way to Carlisle, raising a suffocating dust. At dark the march was resumed, and having proceeded a short distance, we were ordered to discharge our muskets, which had been loaded for the rebels. This made a continuous blaze of light along the whole line. Some of the men charged and fired again, to keep up the sport, but the Colonel put a stop to this. The road grew rougher as we advanced, and many of our comrades now and again stumbled and fell in the darkness. After having marched twelve miles, and arrived within some three miles of Greencastle, we were halted about half-past eight o'clock, and went into camp in the woods. Sleep came without courting. I had never before felt its influence so insinuating, so benumbing, so irresistible!

Monday, September 22. The teams being now dismissed, each man shouldered his own luggage, and the march was resumed at eight o'clock. At Greencastle we found an encampment designated as "Camp M'Cormick," containing several thousand militia, which had not proceeded further south than this point, having been among the later organizations. With these was the 20th Regiment, containing the companies of Captains Boas, Geiger, and Harner, from Reading, with whom we exchanged friendly greetings as we passed. About a mile above Greencastle we were halted in a wood, and after considerable manœuvring, the import of which we could not understand, and, being very tired, could not appreciate, we stacked arms and unslung knapsacks. Here we were rejoined by several of our men who had been down the day before to visit the battle-field, having been fortunate enough to secure passes from the military authorities for that purpose. They gave terrible descriptions of the scenes which they had witnessed, and exhibited a number of relics which they had brought away. It was understood that the parley at this juncture was with reference to the arrangements for transportation, a subject which, as usual, appeared to be involved in much intricacy. The period of our stay in this situation was therefore uncertain, and after dinner had been served, the remainder of the day was given up to relaxation and amusement. Under the latter head came in performances of blanket-tossing and elephant parades—tricks which most of us had never seen before, but which we learned were well known among old soldiers. The Sancho Panza of this occasion was a small boy, picked up by the Lancaster Company, and I dare say that, from the energy and perseverance with which the sport was conducted, the unfortunate lad got more of it than he bargained for. This company had among their number a comical genius named Gable, irreverently dubbed the "Chaplain," whose sallies afforded a never-ending source of amusement to his comrades, as well as to some of the field and staff officers, who frequently formed a portion of his admiring auditory. Most of the Chaplain's wit on this, as on other occasions, was of a character that would have far removed it from the test of refined criticism. Mirth and song filled in the waning hours of the day, and, all restraints being removed, the night was given up to general hilarity.

Tuesday, September 23. Were aroused at 2 A.M. by the receipt of orders to proceed to the railroad, half a mile away, for transportation. Again we were the victims of an unfortunate bungle in the railway arrangements. The train which had been intended for our accommodation was appropriated by another regiment, whose triumphant departure up the valley we had the satisfaction of witnessing. Several other trains passed, and at daylight we were still in statu quo, worn out with fatigue, and vexed with disappointment. The entire day was passed in the same situation, and to add to our discomfiture, the rations had given out and the neighborhood was unpromising for forage of any kind. Was assigned for guard duty the ensuing night from ten to twelve, when lo! at about eleven, after the long expected event had ceased to be anticipated, it came to pass suddenly. The screech of a steam-whistle was heard alongside of us, which announced that our train was at last on hand. After the usual preparatory bustle, we were safely loaded up, and were presently whizzing off at a good speed toward Chambersburg. The dim light of the lanterns tied to the rods at the top of the cars, threw a gloomy air over the sleeping freight which they contained. At one o'clock a halt of an hour was made at Chambersburg, and by daylight Shippensburg was reached.

Wednesday, September 24. At Carlisle another stop of half an hour. The morning was clear and bright, and the men in the most cheerful spirits. We arrived at Harrisburg at eleven o'clock, and were marched at once to the Capitol grounds, where we turned over our arms and accoutrements at the Arsenal. In company with K., I went to the United States Hotel, where we got a good dinner. I am inclined to think the landlord did not clear much on the meal which we laid in on that occasion. At 1.45 P.M. the company took the regular afternoon passenger train for Reading, our Pottsville friends being again with us. Reached home at 4.15, and found a concourse of citizens assembled at the depot with a band of music to receive us. After a short street parade, by way of exhibition, I presume, of the State's gallant defenders, we filed into our old mustering place, at Fifth and Washington Streets, where, with loud and hearty cheers for everybody concerned, we were dismissed, and thus our brief but memorable militia campaign of eleven days peacefully ended.

The company of Captain Bickley, which had been the first to leave Reading, was also the first to reach home. On the day it arrived, a proclamation was issued by Governor Curtin, discharging the militia, with his grateful acknowledgments in the name of the

State, and commending their bravery in passing the borders, although not required to do so by the terms of the call, holding Hagerstown against an advancing foe, and resisting the threatened movement of the rebels upon Williamsport until the United States troops arrived and relieved them. This timely and heroic action, the Governor said, saved the State from the tread of the invading enemy. He recommended that the militia organizations be preserved and perfected—a suggestion which was not generally followed.

The only sad feature of the campaign was the dreadful accident which befel the company of Captain Boas, from Reading, of the 20th Regiment, on the Cumberland Valley Railroad, near Harrisburg, at an early hour on the morning of Friday, the 26th of September. The train on which they were returning collided with one going in the opposite direction, and four members of the company were killed and some thirty injured.

General McClellan thanked Governor Curtin for the timely aid of the State militia, and the moral support thus rendered to the army. Governor Bradford, of Maryland, made a similar acknowledgment. Nearly fifty thousand Pennsylvania militia responded to the original call, about one-half of whom were in actual service on the border. The following year they were compensated by the State, the Legislature having made an appropriation for that purpose, allowing fifteen days' pay to each man, at the rate prescribed by Act of Congress for the payment of the regulars and volunteers in the United States service.

Pennsylvania Governor Andrew Curtain

Maryland Governor Augustus Williamson Bradford

President Lincoln meeting with General McClellan
Sharpsburg, 1862